D1809512

IT Starter Series presents

WORDPRESS FOR BEGINNERS

Learn Everything about WordPress
Websites, Plugins, & SEO

Joseph Conner

About IT Starter Series

IT Starter Series is an independent publishing brand by MJG Publishing OU focusing on non-fiction books. Our eBooks and paperback books are targeting to help individuals to upgrade their careers & lifestyle. Learn new skills & abilities. Find the job of your dreams or create your own freelancing opportunity!

Contact:

Visit our website: http://www.itstarterseries.com/
Email us: contact@itstarterseries.com

Feel free to contact us at any time and we'll personally reply to you.

Free Video Course:
Introduction to JavaScript, SQL & C++

Welcome to the journey into the world of programming. Hi I'm Marco from IT Starter Series, I wanted to thank you for supporting this book.

In it, you'll learn the 3 most in demand programming languages with step-by-step real examples for

- JavaScript;
- SQL ;
- C++.

If you study only ONE of those you can have a good career in programming.

Study all three of these and you'll be highly desired and in demand.

But where do you start? We've built a video course tailored to help you decide.

The **IT Starter Series Free Video Course** will:

- Show you real world code examples to help you decide which is the best fit for you;
- Teach you how to set up the different programming environments;
- Provide step-by-step programming tutorials for immediate action at home.

Follow this link: **http://www.itstarterseries.com/free-programming-course NOW** and get immediate instant access to your free video series!

Access this FREE video course: **http://www.itstarterseries.com/free-programming-course**!

Happy coding!

Want to learn more about programming?

Check out the other books by IT Starter Series:

Newest release (2017): Programming: Computer Programming for Beginners - Learn the Basics of SQL

C#: Programming: Computer Programming for Beginners - Learn the Basics of C# - 3rd Edition (2017)

Programming: Computer Programming for Beginners - Learn the Basics of HTML5, JavaScript and CSS

Hacking: Hacking for Beginners - Computer Virus, Cracking, Malware, IT Security

The Amazon Bestseller: Programming: Computer Programming for Beginners - Learn the Basics of Java, SQL & C++ - 4th Edition (2017)

Check out our **Facebook** (https://www.facebook.com/itstarter series) and **Instagram** (https://www.instagram.com/itstarter series.com) to receive updates on the newest releases!

Table of Contents

Introduction

Are you hoping to learn all about WordPress and how to build your very own website? You must be, otherwise you wouldn't have arrived here. One of the very best things about WordPress is how easy it is to learn and to use. You don't require much money or time, and you can pretty much learn it as you go along. In this guide, I am going to show you how to download and use WordPress to build a website for free, or for very little money, in a very short space of time.

WordPress is the most popular of all the CMSs in the world – that's a Content Management System. That is really just a posh way of saying that you can build a blog or a website with it. More than 20% of all websites on the Internet today are run on WordPress and it is responsible for the generation of thousands of work opportunities the world over. Not only that, millions of WordPress websites are being used to make money, in some cases, some significant amounts of money.

Provided you have a couple of hours to spare each week, you will find it easy to learn WordPress. You do need to have some basic skills in using search engines, like Google, and you must be able to follow instructions. You don't need to know any special skills, like HTML, and you don't need to be a programmer to build your website.

If you are ready to start building, let's start learning WordPress.

Chapter 1:

Setting up WordPress

Before you can even consider building a website, you need to start by installing and setting up WordPress, and this begins with you deciding which version to download – wordpress.org or wordpress.com. Whoa, hold on, there are two versions? Yes there are, and I am going to give you a brief overview of each one so that you can make a decision on the best one to download.

Wordpress.org

This is commonly known as "the real WordPress" and is the one that you hear about most of the time. Wordpress.org is open source and it is completely free, anyone can make use of it. All you will need, and we'll talk more about this in a while, is a domain name and a decent web hosting company – it is often referred to as a self-hosted platform.

Below, we look at the pros and cons of using Wordpress.org to build your website:

Advantages

When you use wordpress.org, you retain complete control over your website. You can do pretty much what you like and you can apply any customization that you like, provided it is WordPress compatible. Other benefits include:

- **Free and dead simple to use**

You will own everything about and on your website; all the data, the content, the website itself. There is no way that your website can be taken down because someone else determines that it doesn't fit their service terms, so long as you do not do anything that could be considered illegal.

- **Add as many WordPress plugins as you want – free, paid, or custom**

Your website design is down to you and much of that will come from WordPress plugins. There are loads to choose from, some free and some paid, including a whole host of themes too. You may also come up with your own custom designs and modify any of the themes to suit you.

- **Make money**

Your WordPress site can be used to make you money and you do this by running ads on it, without the need to share any earnings with any other party.

- **Make use of powerful tracking tools**

Tools like Google Analytics are at your disposal for tracking your website and for analyzing results and statistics.

- **Create an online store**

Your website doesn't have to be like a blog or a content site; you can also add an online store that you sell digital or physical goods and services through; you can set it up to take PayPal payments, credit or debit card payments, and arrange shipping directly through the website.

The Disadvantages

There actually aren't too many disadvantages to using self-hosted WordPress:

- **You still need a web host**

All the files that make up your website are stored with a host and you can start off paying as little as a few dollars a month. But, as your website gets more popular and grows, those costs increase –

by then though, you should be making sufficient income to cover that.

- **Updates are your responsibility**

However, this isn't difficult since wordpress.org contains a simple one-click update button and all you do is click on it.

- **Backups are your responsibility too**

Again, this isn't too difficult as there are loads of WordPress plugins for backups and there is bound to be one that will suit your purposes.

- **The true cost of using wordpress.org will depend on your site**

If you are building a simple blog, then the only costs are the domain name and the web hosting. If, however, you are adding an eCommerce store, for example, there will be other costs involved. You also need to consider the templates – free or premium – and the plugins – again, free or premium.

WordPress.com

WordPress.com was created by Matt Mullenweg, one of the founders of WordPress, which is more of a hosting service. It is because they have the same founder that WordPress.com and WordPress.org tend to be muddled up, but they are very different services. For a start, WordPress.com has five separate plans for you to choose from:

- **Free** – limited service
- **Personal** – costs $36 a year
- **Premium** – costs $99 a year
- **Business** – costs $299 a year
- **VIP** – costs start at $5000 a month

Now let's take a look at the advantages and disadvantages of using WordPress.com:

Advantages:

- **Up to 3 GB space free**

If you want more than that, though, you will need to sign up to a paid plan. The personal plan gives you up to 6 GB, premium up to 13 GB, while the business plan allows you unlimited storage.

- **No need to worry about backups and updates**

WordPress will take care of everything for you, so you don't need to worry.

Disadvantages:

There are limitations to the free plan on WordPress.com and they are what makes it different from WordPress.org:

- **Free plan = ads**

Whether you want them or not, if you take up the free plan on WordPress.com, you will get ads on your websites. Your website users see those ads, but you don't make anything from them. If you don't want your visitors to see the WordPress ads, you will need to upgrade to a paid plan.

- **You can't sell ads**

WordPress.com does not allow you sell ads on your site. However, if your website is high traffic, you can put in an application to join WordAds, their own advertising program, where any revenue is shared. Business and premium users can go straight onto it.

- **You cannot upload any plugins**

If you have a free plan, you will automatically get pre-activated JetPack features built in. If you have a business plan, you will be given a choice of compatible plugins to choose from, but, if you have the VIP plan, you can install as many plugins as you like.

- **No custom themes either**

You also can't upload any custom themes. If you have the free plan, you get a few free themes to choose from – not many, though – and business and premium users get a choice of premium themes.

- **Limited customization**

Free plan owners can't do much in the way of customization, but the business and premium users get access to custom CSS.

- **Stats are restricted**

You can only use the WordPress stats, not Google Analytics or any of the other truly powerful tracking and analysis options. Only business plan owners can use Google Analytics.

- **Your site can be deleted at any time**

Although this will only happen if WordPress believes that their Terms of Service have been violated in any way.

- **A "Powered by WordPress.com" link will be on your site**

The only way to remove this is to upgrade your plan to the Business plan.

Finally, you cannot use any integrated payment gateway or eCommerce features. Nor can you build up any membership-type features.

When you compare the two, WordPress.com is rather limited unless you are prepared to pay big bucks for a Premium or VIP plan. So, why could it be best for you? If your website is a personal blog or you are not fussed whether your website makes you any money, then sign up to the free WordPress.com plan. If, however, you are looking to make money or you are running a business, go for the WordPress.org option – you get more freedom and the ability to let your website grow in as many different ways as you want.

You could fork over $299 a year for a business plan on WordPress.com, and that price is for each website; your money will go a whole lot further if you use WordPRess.org and pay out approximately $46 per year for hosting.

To be fair, WordPress.org is the much better platform to choose and is the one that most of the professional bloggers and many of the largest business websites in the world are built on, including Disney.

Chapter 2:

Get Your Domain Name

and Web Hosting

One of the most crucial factors for the success of your website is the domain name. Choosing the wrong one will do you no favors at all, and it isn't easy to change it later on without damaging your search rank and your brand. You must choose the right name at the start, so I am going to give you the best 8 tips for choosing the right name:

1. Go with a .com domain

There are loads of name extensions to choose from and lots of new ones appear on a regular basis. Choose a domain name with one of the original extensions, preferably .com. You could be very creative and come up with some clever names for your website using new extensions, but the .com extension is still the most respected and credible one, not to mention the most firmly established. Not all the new extensions can be trusted and many will never be remembered, whereas .com will always be in everyone's memories and is the one most likely to be typed. And anyway, many of the smartphone and tablet devices already have a .com button!

2. Always use keywords

I will be covering this in more detail later when we talk about SEO (Search Engine Optimization) but, for now, it is enough for you to understand that keywords are incredibly important. When you use the right keywords in your domain name, you are informing the search engines of the topic of your website. Add quality content to that, along with a great experience for users on your site and using keywords will help you rise higher in the Google rankings.

It won't be easy to find a really good domain name that has your keywords in it and is still available, so you need to get a bit creative. Mix your keywords with other words to give your website a name that truly stands out.

3. Keep your domain name short

Keywords are very important but you mustn't make your domain name too long. Keep it short and keep it memorable. Less than 15 characters is generally a good idea because the longer names are not so easy to remember, and your users are more likely to make a mistake when typing them in as well – that can change significant amounts of traffic.

4. Easy to spell, easy to pronounce

Don't ever make your domain name difficult to spell or to say – it should flow as easily when you say it as when you write it. If someone asks you for that domain name and it is too difficult to remember, that's another lost opportunity for traffic.

5. Keep your domain name brandable and unique

It goes without saying that the domain name should be unique – not only will it stand out, you rest assured of traffic coming to your blog or website and not to someone else's. Do some research into your niche and see what domain names are being used by people with similar products, and also to make sure that you won't be using a name that may be trademarked.

You can also make sure that you choose a name that is brandable – these are catchy, they are unique, and they will be remembered.

6. Don't use hyphens

Do not use hyphens in your domain name because they are generally a signal that the domain is spam and that is not something you want to be associated with – it just gives out the wrong impression.

Not only that, but a name that has one or more hyphens in it is also more susceptible to being mistyped. If the name you want is taken and you choose a similar one with hyphens in it, you could lose traffic if a visitor misses those hyphens out.

7. Don't double your letters

Try to avoid using doubled letters in your domain names – once again, it comes down to those typos. For example, if there were a domain name of WordPresssetup, it would result in far more typos and there would be a lot of lost traffic

8. Don't limit yourself

While you should always choose a name that fits your business, you must not limit yourself. Let's say you are a florist and you choose a name like rosesblog.com. What if you wanted to then start talking about the types of flowers that you sell? You could miss out on valuable traffic because you won't attract visitors who have an interest in flowers, so be sensible about your name.

WordPress Web Hosting

The next most important thing, another one that gets overlooked so much, is web hosting. Without a decent web host, you can put as much effort into your website as you like; it won't get you very far.

Making sure you have the best web host for your requirements can significantly improve SEO and traffic that leads to potential sales. There are lots of hosting options and we are going to look at some of the very best now. We have looked at everything you need to consider when choosing your web host company and the following are the top ones in use today for both service and quality.

1. Bluehost

Bluehost began back in 1996, and is one of the oldest web hosts in existence today. It is also the brand name for WordPress hosting and is the recommended official hosting provider.

When you use Bluehost, there is no need for you to worry about a slow website, even when there are significant amounts of traffic. Their support is offered by experts on a 24/7 basis, be it by email, live chat, or phone. Even better, they have been rated as the number one web host of choice for the small business.

2. HostGator

HostGator is responsible for hosting more than 8 million domains and is another of the most popular hosting providers of all time. It includes one-click installation for WordPress and has an uptime guarantee of 99.9%. Add to that the customer support that operates 24/7 and HostGator becomes a smart choice.

3. SiteGround

SiteGround is another very popular web host provider among the WordPress community, providing in-house security and speed solutions that are unique and give you peace of mind and a secure, fast website. They have the best customer service support in the industry and are classed as an official and recommended hosting site for WordPress users. They also have the automatic upgrades, one-click staging, WordPress caching built-in and GIT version control. Finally, they offer the unique service of hosting that is location specific with servers in Europe, the USA, and Asia.

4. InMotion Hosting

InMotion Hosting is an industry brand that is well known for reliability in performance, specifically for hosting in the business class. Its technical support has won awards and they guarantee an uptime of 99.9%, making them a favorite among users. Their support is based in the USA and is unmatched by any other hosting provider.

5. DreamHost

Like Bluehost, DreamHost is another long-standing hosting provider, having been around for more than 21 years. They are well known for making your web hosting experience simple and providing you with tools and features like one-click installation of WordPress, automatic updating, unlimited storage space, free SSD's to make your website run up to 200% faster, and unlimited bandwidth. They are responsible for hosting more than half a million websites and blogs, charge you no fees for setup, and give you a free domain name.

So, there you have the top 5 web hosting providers for WordPress users; although there are many more, they cannot match the level of support that any of these five offers you and, for a beginner, you should make your choice from these. It is worth noting that, although some providers offer free domain names, it may still be better to do this separately.

Chapter 3:

Build Your WordPress Website

Starting your very first website can be a scary thing, especially when you have little experience at technical things. You're not the only one but, when you use WordPress, setting up a blog or a website is dead simple and I'm going to walk you through it now, step by step, from start to finish. Some of what is in this chapter will only be briefly covered because we already covered it in more detail in previous chapters, so please refer back where necessary. Ready?

Before we begin, here are the answers to some of the more frequent questions.

1. What will I need to build a website?

There are three things you will need to begin a WordPress website:

- Your domain name – see chapter two, this is the name of your website
- WordPress hosting – again, see chapter two for more details.
- About 45 minutes to an hour of uninterrupted time

Seriously, that is all it will take to build your very first website with WordPress.

2. How much will it cost me?

That depends entirely on what sort of website you are going to build. Typically, a business website can cost anything from $100 a year right up to $30,000 or more. You should start small and build your website up as your business builds up. Don't try to do it all at once; it will cost a lot more and is almost doomed to failure from the word go. I'm going to walk you through building a website that costs less than $100.

3. Which is the best platform for building a website?

There are loads of different builders that will help you with your website but we're going to use WordPress, the self-hosted version. It is the most popular and it is the easiest to use. WordPress.org is free to use and is packed with thousands of different extensions and designs for your website. It is one of the most flexible of all website builders and it is compatible with virtually all third-party services and tools available to you.

Getting the Most Out of This Guide

This is a guide for building a website. It has been divided into sections to make it easier to follow and I will walk you through it all, one step at a time. Just follow the guide carefully and the result will be a nice, professional website. So, have fun with this and see what you can create. Let's start.

Step One – The Setup

One of the biggest mistakes made by beginners is not using the right platform to build their website with, but as you are reading this guide, clearly you have chosen WordPress, the very best one to use. For the majority of users, WordPress.org is the best solution, simply because it has everything that you need, including untold numbers of designs and add-ons that will make your website truly unique. And, it's free, which is always a great reason to try something; it can also be used to build websites of all kinds with no restrictions.

The reason it is free is that it is self-hosted, which means you need to purchase your own domain name and your own web hosting – these are not free. Typically, you can expect to pay around $9.99 or more per year for your domain name and you can get hosting from about $7.99 a month. Sometimes, you will see offers from web hosting platforms but beware; they may be cheap, but they may not offer everything you need and there may be hidden costs involved.

For this guide, we are going to use Bluehost, one of the official partners for WordPress hosting and they are providing a special introductory offer of a free domain name and web hosting for just $2.95 per month. They also offer a 30-day money back guarantee, free site builders, and 24/7 customer support.

So, your first step is to buy your domain name and your hosting package. To do this, head over to the Bluehost website and click the big green button that says, "Get Started Now". A new page with details of pricing will open and here you have a choice of three plans:

- Basic – normally $7.99 per month, introductory offer of $2.95
- Plus – normally $10.99 per month, introductory offer of $5.49
- Prime – normally $14.99 per month, introductory offer of $5.49

The prices revert to normal upon renewal so keep this in mind.

Choose the plan that suits your purposes and click on "Select". This will take you to the next page where you get to choose your domain name. Now hopefully you followed the last chapter and have already worked out a domain name, but you do need to have several in reserve – the chances of your first choice being available are quite slim.

If you haven't done this yet, stick to .com, make your name short, related to your business, easy to spell, easy to pronounce, and memorable. Input your chosen name and then click "Next".

Here, you will be asked to input your personal details for your account, like your name, physical address, and email address. And you will also be given a choice of some optional extras that you may want to purchase. At this stage, do NOT purchase any of them; you can add them in later if you really need them. Finally, to complete the purchase of your package, enter your payment information.

You will now get an email that tells you how to login to cPanel – this is your control panel for Bluehost. This is your dashboard, and is where you manage your website, get support, set up your email accounts, and everything else that relates to your website. Oh yes, and this is where you install WordPress from.

Step Two: Installing WordPress

When you first look at your dashboard, you will find loads of different icons, all allowing you to do different things. It's safe to say that you will most likely not use any more than about 5% of them so don't worry about them for now.

So, go down the page to the Website section and look for the WordPress icon – click on it. A new screen will appear; this is the Bluehost MarketPlace Quick Install. Simply click the button that says, "Get Started".

Next, you will need to choose the domain name where WordPress is to be installed. Click on the drop-down menu and then click the domain name; click "Next".

Type in the name of your website, your admin username, and then a password for the website. You can change these later on if you want in WordPress settings. Make sure there is a tick in every checkbox you see on the screen and then you can click on "Install" to continue.

Now Quick Install will begin the process of installing WordPress onto the chosen website. While the installation process completes, you will see a series of web templates that you can use on your website. Don't worry about these for now; later on, we are going to look at locating and installing free templates.

When the installation has finished, the top header will show a success message so click on the link that reads "Installation Complete" and you will be taken to the WordPress login screen.

Congratulations! You have just created a website using WordPress! See how simple it was?

You will need to input your login URL and it will look something like this:

http://www.yourdomain.com/wp-admin

Earlier, you were asked to set a password for the admin username; use this username and password to enter your WordPress site. That was easy, wasn't it? Now we need to move on and start designing your website.

Step Three: Choosing a Theme

How your website looks is down to the WordPress theme that you choose. These themes are templates, designed professionally, that you install to change the appearance of your website. By default, every WordPress website will have a basic theme and you can see that just by visiting your website. Go and do that now and then come back.

Doesn't look too brilliant does it! Not to worry because you have thousands of themes to choose from, some paid and some free. To change the theme of your website, you need to go to your WordPress dashboard, so go there now and click on the option for "Appearance" and then click on "Themes". Now click the button that says, "Add New".

A new screen will appear and here you can search through almost 4500 free themes, all stored in the official themes directory for WordPRess.org. Here, you can sort them using various filters, including 'featured', 'popular', 'latest', 'layout' and many other filters. For this guide, we are going to be using one called 'Bento", but later you can change it to any other one that you want. Bento is a very popular, multi-purpose theme with plenty of design options to suit all kinds of websites. Type the name into the search field and then run your mouse over the name of the theme and click on "Install".

As soon as the theme has installed, you can begin to customize it by clicking on the link for "Customize". You will find it under the menu for "Appearance". The customizer will now be launched and here you can make the changes you want, using a live preview

– this shows your website in real-time as you change settings, so you can see what they look like.

There isn't any need to do everything on here right now; you will find it much easier to customize the website once you have got some content on it.

Step Four: Adding Some Content to Your Website

There are two default types of content on WordPress – Pages and Posts. Posts are to do with blogs and will appear in a reverse-chronological order, i.e. the newest posts appear first. Pages, on the other hand, are static and are for one-off bits of content, like your Contacts page, your About Me page, and your Privacy Policy.

By default, WordPress will show blog posts on the first page of the website. That can be changed, however, and you can get WordPress to show any chosen page as the front page. We'll look at that later but first, we are going to put some content onto your website.

Let's begin by adding some pages to the website. It really doesn't matter if you have insufficient content to fill these pages right now; we can edit them and update later.

Head on over the admin area of your WordPress dashboard and click on "Pages" and then on "Add New Page". You will now see an editor screen for the page. The first thing you need to do is give the page a title so, for now, we'll call this one "Home".

The next step is to put some content into the page editor and here, you can add some text, links, add a few images, embed video links or audio, and so on. Once you have added some content, click the button that says "Publish" and it will be live, showing on your website. Go ahead and see how it looks.

You can do this for as many pages as you want, add in some different website sections, such as a blog page, the About and Contact Us Pages, for example. Let's input some blog posts.

To do this, in your WordPress admin section, click on "Posts" and then on "Add New", in much the same way as you did for the Pages. A screen will appear, this is the Blog Editor and it looks like the Page Editor you used earlier.

Input a title for the post and then your content. There are also a few other options to choose from, like Categories, Post Format, and Tags.

Once you have finished with the editor, you have two choices – click on "Save" and the post will be stored as a draft (this means you can make changes to it before publishing) or you can click on "Publish" and the post will be instantly uploaded and live on your website.

Now you know how to add content, it's time to do a bit of tweaking to your website.

Step Five: Tweak and Customize Your Website

Let's put all your content into a neat format on your website, one that will look appealing and will make your website user-friendly. We'll start by making a static front page. To do this, from the admin area, click on "Settings" and then on "Read Me". You will see an option that says, "Front Page Displays"; click it and then click on the option for "Static Front Page". Now choose "Pages" and you can choose the Home and the Blog pages you created earlier. Now click on the button that says, "Save Changes" and WordPress will now show your Home page as the front page of your website and the Blog page will show all your blog posts.

Next, we want to change the title and the tagline of your site. When you installed WordPress, you chose a title for the website and WordPress added a tagline automatically to that title. That tagline just says, "Just another WordPress site" so we need to change the title and the tagline. To do this, go to "Settings" and then click on "General".

The site title is your website name and the tagline is generally one line describing the website. You can, if you want, leave the field for the tag line blank.

Do what you need to do and then click the "Save Changes" button.

Just a couple more things to do. First, let's set up the settings for Comments. WordPress has an automatic comments system built in, and this is what lets your visitors comment on posts that you publish. While this is a great way of engaging with your users, it is also a magnet for spammers. To sort this out, you must enable moderation for comments on your website.

Go to the "Settings" and then click on "Discussions". From there, go down to where it says, "Before a Comment Appears" and click the box next to the option for "Comment must be manually approved".

Again, click on the button for "Save Changes" so your changes are all stored.

Lastly, we are going to create a navigation menu on your website. These menus let your users move around your website, looking at the different pages and sections. WordPress has a very powerful system for this and the WordPress theme you chose (Bento) uses this system to display those menus.

First, go to "Appearance" and then click on "Menus". Input a name for the menu and then click on the button that says, "Create Menu". Your new navigation menu is now going to be created by WordPress but, to start with, there won't be anything in it.

So, choose which of your pages you want to show up in the navigation menu and, for each one, click on the button that says, "Add to Menu". Each of your chosen pages will start to appear in the navigation menu and you can position them in the order you want them in by moving them up or down.

When you have them in the order you want, you need to choose a display location. These are dependent on the theme you chose but most will have a Primary menu. Choose where you want them and then click on "Menu".

Head over to your website and see what all your changes have done. How does it look now?

Like it? Now you can go back and make any changes you want, add any content you want and build up your website as you see fit.

For the final chapters, we will be looking at some of the best plugins for your WordPress website and how to use SEO to optimize your website for the search engine results, specifically Google.

Chapter 4:
The Very Best WordPress Plugins

Plugins are an excellent way of adding functionality to your website. There are more than 47,000 plugins stored in the official WordPress repository for plugins to suit every feature or function you could possibly want. Although what you use will depend on the niche your website is in, there are some that should be on all websites. To make things a little easier for you, I have dug out some of the best free and paid plugins or every website.

1. Jetpack – free

Jetpack is a very powerful plugin and is packed with features that look after the security of your website, performance, optimization of your images, traffic growth, the appearance of the website, and a whole lot more. An enhanced distribution feature shares the content you publish automatically to search engines and other third-party services; this is what will increase your traffic. It will also create a sitemap so that Google and other engines can index your website easily. Its best feature is the security it offers in the prevention of brute force attacks. Your website is monitored in 5-minute intervals for downtime and you will be notified instantly of any problems.

2. Akismet – freemium

Akismet is another powerful plugin and is a default one that comes with all new core installations of WordPress. This plugin prevents spam, checking every comment and filtering the spam comments out. Every comment will have a status history so you can see which ones the moderator or Akismet determined to be spam. Moderators may also see how many approved comments there are for each of the users, view any URL's that appear in the body of the content, and remove any that are suspicious.

If you have a blog or a personal website, Akismet is free, but if you are running a commercial site, you will need to pay a monthly premium. These premium plans also provide you with added security.

3. Yoast SEO – freemium

Search engines are the biggest source of traffic for any website and this is why SEO is important. Yoast SEO is your guide to creating better content and making your search engine rankings much better. Yoast is focused on making your content useful and SEO-friendly, starting with choosing a focus keyword and ensuring that it is properly used in the content you are writing. A feature for page analysis will make sure that keyword has been used everywhere it needs to be and it will also suggest a better way for your content to be set out for the search engines.

4. Google XML Sitemaps – free

This is another of the SEO plugins and it assists the search engines to index your site by using an XML sitemap. When the plugin is activated, an XML sitemap will be created for your website, which makes it much easier to be indexed. The sitemap lets the search bots see how your website is structured and is more efficient at getting results. And, every time you publish new content on your website, the plugin will tell all of the big search engines.

5. All in One Schema.org Rich Snippets – free

When you look at the pages on the search results, have you ever noticed things like star ratings, how many reviews, or images? These give you more information about a post or a page and they are called Rich Snippets. These are a great way of making your page or post look better on the search engine results and can provide major bits of information about your page or product, giving you better click through rates.

This plugin will give the search engines all the information needed to be shown in the results pages, thus providing better opportunities for ranking.

6. W3 Cache – freemium

A great way of improving the performance of your website is to use WordPress caching. The website data is stored in the cache temporarily so that, when the user opens the page again next time, it loads much faster.

W3 Cache is one of the best plugins for this, featuring page cache, object cache, database cache, browser cache, and a whole lot more besides. It also helps to cut down the page-load times by integrating CDN services and offers HTTP compression of your CSS, JS and HTML files, saving up to 80% bandwidth. All of this increases your search engine rankings and attracts more traffic and potential conversions.

7. WP Smush – freemium

Images are fantastic for your website because they are attention grabbers and they often get your message across much quicker than a post can. They also make your pages look good and are engaging. However, they also take up space and can slow your website down and that is the last thing you want. The WP Smush plugin compresses your images and optimizes them without compromising their quality. It works on all GIF, JPEG, and PNG file formats using advanced techniques and saves you a ton of storage space. It will automatically smush attachments as they are uploaded, and you can smush in bulk as well.

8. WP-Optimize – free

WP-Optimize is an excellent plugin to help clean the WordPress database and optimize it. It will get rid of any unnecessary data and keep your database fully optimized for top performance. There may be a whole heap of unwanted data hanging about on your website that you won't even know about, and this plugin will sort it all out for you, removing spam comments, those that have not been approved, trash, pingbacks, trackbacks, and a whole lot more.

9. BJ Lazy Load – free

When you use loads of images on your website, they can slow down load times and cause problems for you and your users. WordPress has a solution for everything and in this case, we have a plugin called BJ Lazy Load.

It will take all the images on your website, be they in posts, gravatars, thumbnails or iFrames for content and replace them all with placeholders. Then, as the content nears time to enter the browser screen, it will load them. When a user scrolls down the page, it will display the images, speeding up your loading times and saving on bandwidth.

10. WordFence Security – freemium

One of the most important things that you need to do is keep your website secure against hackers. The Internet is full of malicious bots and these can attack without warning at any time, destroying all your hard work.

There are lots of security plugins for WordPress and one of the best is WordFence Security. It has lots of features, including malware scans, firewall protection, login security, blocking, monitoring of live traffic, and a good deal more. When you monitor the traffic to your website in real time, you can be more aware of any security threats and take the appropriate action.

The firewall application stops your website from being hacked and blocking will stop all known attackers. Two-factor authentication is included for login security and all passwords, for both admin and users, are checked for strength.

11. Broken Link Checker – free

This one is self-explanatory. While you might have a fantastic website with lots of regular traffic, have you ever considered what would happen if your users kept landing on broken links? It's pretty obvious, you will lose customers.

This little plugin will keep an eye on your website for broken links and tells you if it finds any. It will also tell you if there are any images missing so that you can fix things quickly. This plugin also contains options that stop the search engines from following any of the broken links.

12. Redirection – free

Sometimes you will need to make changes to your post or page permalinks, but you might forget that they need to be redirected afterward. When this happens, visitors will be sent to a "Not Available" page because the URL they are following no longer exists. Redirection is a great plugin for managing 301 redirections and tracking any 404 errors. When you change the URL of a post the plugin adds a redirection automatically and provides you with a log for each one. This is a useful plugin for when you want to migrate pages to a new website.

13. MailChimp for WordPress – Freemium

MailChimp is an incredibly popular marketing service that manages email subscribers, sends bulk emails, and tracks the results. Integrating this into your website is simple when you use the MailChimp WordPress plugin, and it lets you add subscription forms to your blog. There is a premium version if you want to use it commercially.

14. Social Icons – free

There is no argument that social media is a highly populated platform, with user numbers increasing year by year. So, it makes sense that social media should be a part of your website, especially social media marketing. And that's where plugins like Social Icons come in. This will give you a simple way to display the most popular of the social media icons on your site, via short codes or widgets. There are more than 100 social media platforms included and you choose which ones you want.

15. Disable Comments – free

Disable Comments is a useful plugin for you to disable commenting on your website as a whole or on specific post or pages. This cuts down on the amount of spam coming into your website in an easy and manageable way. The plugin also gives you the ability to remove any items related to comments from the Dashboard, the Admin bar, the Admin menu, and Widgets.

While there are thousands of plugins to choose from, these are the best ones for any website, providing you with basic features, toughening up your security, improving speed and SEO, plus helping you to market your website better.

Chapter 5:
WordPress SEO – Optimizing
Your Website

With more than 50 million blog and websites hosted on WordPress.org alone, it's difficult to make one stand out from the rest. You want your website to be the best, to be the one that attracts the trafficm and the best way to do that is to optimize your website. That means SEO, or Search Engine Optimization. In this last chapter, we are going to look at the options you have for using SEO on your website.

URL's

The most important thing is to get your website right, preferably at the time you build it because it is much harder to fix it later on. It is also imperative if you want the search engines to notice you, as well as potential visitors. One of the best ways to do this is to have a clear URL structure.

Your URL should have a couple of keywords in it that are related to your page content. All search engines want to see relevancy and using keywords is the best way to show them this. By default, your post permalinks will not be attractive and will generally contain numbers, something like this:

http://housesforu.com//?p=123.

This is not what search engines want to see because it doesn't really tell them anything. It doesn't mean anything to potential visitors either, so you need to change their structure. Click on "Settings" and then "Permalinks" on your dashboard and you will see several structure types. Now it's down to you. The default will always have numbers but clicking on "Custom Structure" will let you set your own. You could have a category name in your URL, for example:

http://housesforu/London/maisonette

While others say you should just have the name of the post:

http://housesforu/maisonette

Whichever way you choose, don't use more than five keywords – search engines don't like it.

Sitemaps

Some websites have literally hundreds of pages and that can make it difficult to get them indexed by the search engines. To deal with this, you need to tell that search engine what your website structure is and you do that by creating a sitemap. The Google XML Sitemap plugin will generate one for you automatically and tell the search engines so they know where to look.

Google Analytics

This is one of the most popular and useful of all the analysis tools and is owned by Google. You can use it for free and it helps you to track traffic to your website. It tells you where the traffic comes from, how it behaves, and lots of other important information that will help you reach your audience. It will help you find 404 error pages and fight against spam from referrals as well.

SEO Themes

WordPress offers loads of themes, but rather than just choosing one that looks nice, you should also choose one that has already been optimized for the search engines. These themes have two main factors – code and speed. Themes that are written properly will include all the latest best practices for SEO, and this will guarantee that the search bots will find the right code among all the source code. Some of the most important factors to consider are:

SEO Plugins

WordPress also has thousands of plugins to choose from and many of these are SEO plugins. These will look after your website and will prompt you to add the right Meta titles, descriptions, tags, keywords, and a whole lot more besides. Plugins like Yoast offer a total WordPress SEO solution.

Media Optimization

Media is one of the most important parts of your website, but depending on how you do this, media can improve or destroy your efforts at SEO. Naming and tagging images are important but how you do it is even more important. With the correct tagging, your chances of a higher search engine ranking or images are much better.

It isn't enough to upload an image with a name, and using complex names simply isn't good practice when it comes to SEO. When you upload your images, you are given options to change titles, add captions, descriptions, and alt text. Use these options to push your website further up the rankings.

Shareable Content

Social media is here to stay; platforms like Twitter, Facebook, Google+ and LinkedIn are among the most used with millions of users. Allowing your content to be shared on these platforms will give your website a huge boost and drive significant amounts of traffic to you as well as giving your website huge amounts of credibility.

Anchor Text and Links

Most likely, you already know that having links in your posts is very important, but what you may not be aware of is how your links can be optimized. First and foremost, include links to your own content. Many website owners forget to do this; interlinking is the quickest way to push your SEO efforts high as well as giving your users a much better experience. However, you should not link just for the sake of linking.

As time has evolved, the search engines have gotten better. They now use more metrics to regulate search rankings and the relevancy of the links is one metric that stands out way above the others. This is determined by source page content and by anchor text. While overuse of anchor text can get your site penalized, done right it can also boost your rankings.

Anchor text is all about linking to content that is relevant to your post and gives your users more information without you needing to write reams and reams of content. Use enough to make it worthwhile but not so many that your post is overloaded, and make sure they are relevant.

High Quality Content

Your content is the most important factor in SEO, so it is important to make sure that it is high quality, highly relevant, and engaging. It really doesn't matter whether you are running a blog or a corporate website; the principle is the same. High quality content will get you noticed by the search engines in the way that you want to be noticed. This kind of content is not only free of grammatical and spelling errors, it is also:

- **Unique** – Google does not like people who steal other peoples' content, and will not hesitate to punish you if you do it. There is nothing wrong with quoting a source in your content and attributing it to the original author, but there is everything wrong with stealing the entire article and using it as your own. Write on the same topics, by all means, and even use the same ideas, but use your own words and put your own take on it to keep it unique.
- **Shareable** – I mentioned this earlier; make sure that your posts can be shared on social media.
- **Informative, helpful, and actionable** – When people are looking for information on the Internet, they are looking for information that is helpful and valuable. One key to SEO success is giving them exactly what they want. Write posts that are informative, write helpful tutorials, write about things you have learned; all of these are truly helpful because they can help your visitors to learn something or fix a problem they may have.

The Right Heading Tags

Where SEO is concerned, one of the biggest best practices to follow is the correct use of heading tags. For those new to all this, you may not even know what a heading tag is, let alone know how to use it in the right way. You will see these tags in the editor and you can choose heading 1 right through to heading 6, but how do you know which ones to use?

The H1 tag is always to be used for the title of the page or post, and this must be a clear and very informative tag. It will tell your readers exactly what they are going to be reading about and it needs to grab their attention.

Next is H2 for extra headings and then you use H3 and so on for the sub headings. Using these right is important for the SEO success of your website and to improve user engagement, because it tells your visitors what it's all about.

SEO Plugins

It doesn't matter whether you are an SEO expert, an amateur, or a complete beginner, SEO plugins in WordPress are some of the best ways to achieve the very best practice in SEO. Using the right ones will give you the ability to add the right information instead of trying to add the Sitemaps, Meta descriptions, and all the other important stuff manually. Two of the very best to use are:

- **Yoast -** This has grown incredibly popular in recent times. It lets you pay better attention to focus keywords in your content as well as helping you to add all the other information. You get a page analysis feature as well.
- **SEO Friendly Images** – This one helps you to optimize all your images for better SEO while also pushing more significant traffic your way from the search engines. You can integrate the ALT attributes in your images, but you do need to come up with your own names.

There is so much to WordPress SEO that I couldn't possibly fit it all into one chapter. The techniques mentioned here are the best and will help you to achieve top results. You need to give your website and your content the absolute best chance possible to be near or at the top of the page ranking. Using these tips will put you a long way forward on your journey as well as bringing in the right traffic; targeted traffic with a much higher chance of conversion to your website. And that is what it is all about at the end of the day.

Conclusion

Well, that's the end of this particular journey, and you should now have the basic skills under your belt to build your own website using WordPress. As you have seen, WordPress is simple to use just as promised, provided you can follow simple instructions and are prepared to put in a couple of hours each week to learn it.

Your next step is to build on what you have learned. If you have got a website up and running then work on it in WordPress and make it better. Play about with WordPress itself, see what you can do with it and learn what all the features can do for you. WordPress also has a great help section and an enormous community where you can go for any questions you have.

Thank you for taking the time to read my guide, I hope you found it helpful and I hope that yours will be the next successful website that I come across in my travels!

Free Video Course:
Introduction to JavaScript, SQL & C++

We really hope that you enjoyed the book! You are now familiar with the first steps on Computer Programming. It's now time to take action!

Follow this link: **http://www.itstarterseries.com/free-programming-course NOW** and get immediate access to your free video series!

Happy coding!

Want to learn more about programming?

Check out the other books by IT Starter Series:

Newest release (2017): **Programming: Computer Programming for Beginners - Learn the Basics of SQL**

C#: Programming: Computer Programming for Beginners - Learn the Basics of C# - 3rd Edition (2017)

Programming: Computer Programming for Beginners - Learn the Basics of HTML5, JavaScript and CSS

Hacking: Hacking for Beginners - Computer Virus, Cracking, Malware, IT Security

The Amazon Bestseller: Programming: Computer Programming for Beginners - Learn the Basics of Java, SQL & C++ - 4th Edition (2017)

Check out our **Facebook** (https://www.facebook.com/itstarter series) and **Instagram** (https://www.instagram.com/itstarter series.com) to receive updates on the newest releases!

Printed in Great Britain
by Amazon